U.S. Fish & Wildlife Service

2006 Eelgrass Survey for Eastern Long Island Sound Connecticut and New York

This page is intentionally blank.

2006 Eelgrass Survey for Eastern Long Island Sound, Connecticut and New York

Ralph Tiner[1], Herb Bergquist[1], Tom Halavik[2] and Andrew MacLachlan[2]

[1]U.S. Fish and Wildlife Service
National Wetlands Inventory Program
Northeast Region
300 Westgate Center Drive
Hadley, MA 01035

[2]U.S. Fish and Wildlife Service
Southern New England Coastal Program
50 Bend Road
Charlestown, RI 02813

Prepared for:

U.S. Environmental Protection Agency
Office of Ecosystem Protection
Region I
Boston, MA

National Wetlands Inventory Report

March 2007

This report should be cited as:

Table of Contents

Appendix. Maps showing distribution of eelgrass beds located during this inventory.

This page is intentionally blank.

Introduction

The U.S. Fish and Wildlife Service's National Wetlands Inventory Program (NWI) is the nation's leader in wetland mapping. To date, wetland maps have been produced for over 90% of the coterminous United States. In 2001, the State of Connecticut's Office of Long Island Sound Programs approached the Service about doing a special inventory of eelgrass in Long Island Sound. The Service initiated this study in 2002 and produced a report on the distribution of eelgrass beds in the eastern portion of Long Island Sound: "Eelgrass Survey for Eastern Long Island Sound, Connecticut and New York" (Tiner, et al. 2003). This survey was intended to be the baseline study for monitoring the status of eelgrass in this area of Long Island Sound.

In 2004, the U.S. Environmental Protection Agency provided funding to update this survey in 2005. This report outlines the methods used in the survey, summarizes inventory results, compares the findings with the 2002 survey, and provides detailed maps showing the location of eelgrass (*Zostera marina*) beds detected during the 2006 survey.

Study Area

The project area encompasses the eastern end of Long Island Sound, including Fishers Island and the North Fork of Long Island (Figure 1). It included all coastal embayments and nearshore waters (i.e., to a depth of –15 feet at mean low water) bordering the Sound from Clinton Harbor to the Rhode Island border and including Fishers Island and the North Shore of Long Island from Southold to Orient Point and Plum Island. The study area includes the tidal zone of 18 sub-basins in Connecticut: Little Narragansett Bay, Stonington Harbor, Quiambog Cove, Mystic Harbor, Palmer-West Cove, Mumford Cove, Paquonock River, New London Harbor, Goshen Cove, Jordan Cove, Niantic Bay, Rocky Neck State Park, Old Lyme Shores, Connecticut River, Willard Bay, Westbrook Harbor, Duck Island Roads, and Clinton Harbor, and two areas in New York: Fishers Island and a portion of the North Shore of Long Island.

Figure 1. Location of eelgrass survey study area, with coastal sub-basins identified.

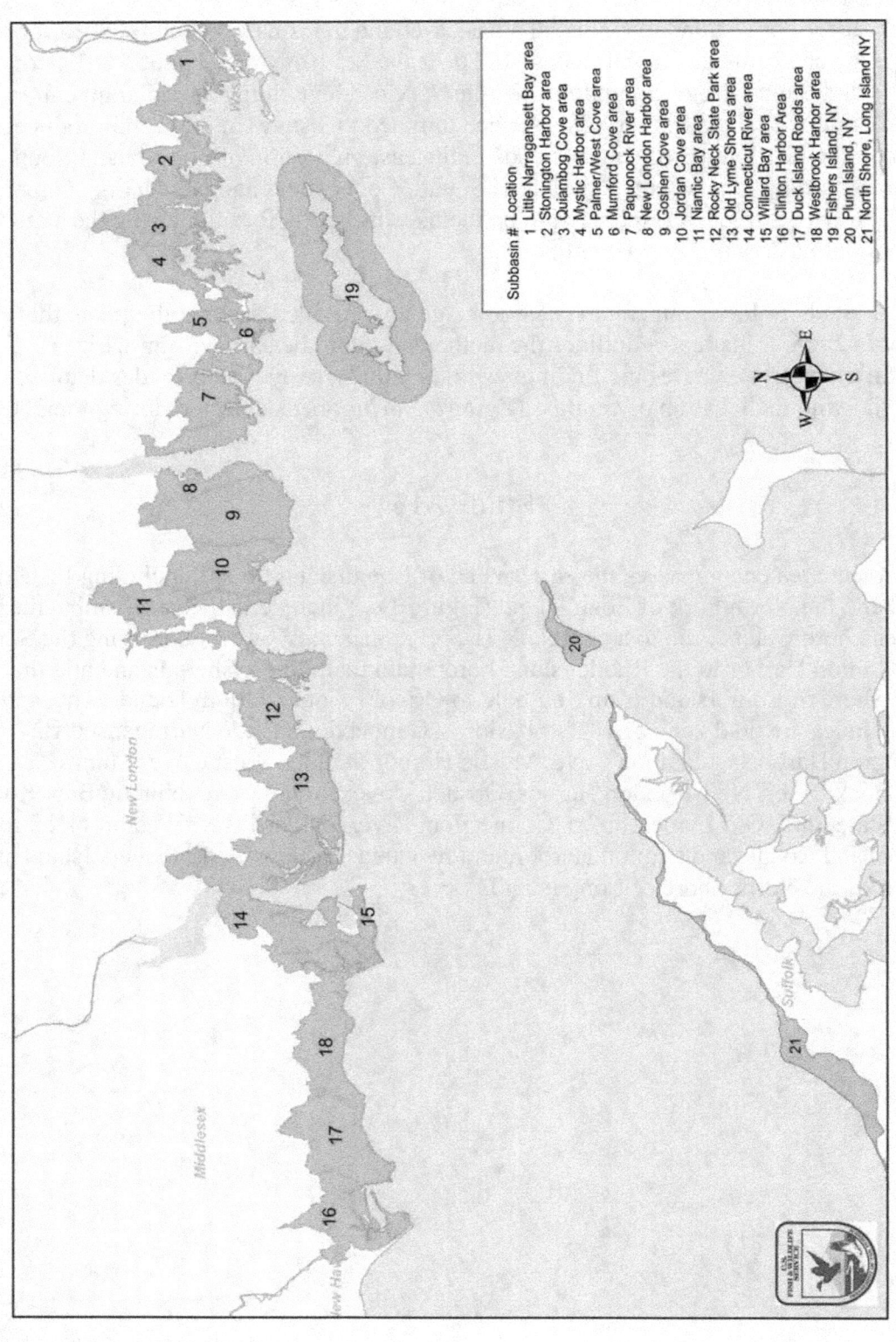

Subbasin # Location
1 Little Narragansett Bay area
2 Stonington Harbor area
3 Quiambog Cove area
4 Mystic Harbor area
5 Palmer/West Cove area
6 Mumford Cove area
7 Paquonock River area
8 New London Harbor area
9 Goshen Cove area
10 Jordan Cove area
11 Niantic Bay area
12 Rocky Neck State Park area
13 Old Lyme Shores area
14 Connecticut River area
15 Willard Bay area
16 Clinton Harbor Area
17 Duck Island Roads area
18 Westbrook Harbor area
19 Fishers Island, NY
20 Plum Island, NY
21 North Shore, Long Island NY

Methods

Acquisition of Aerial Photography

The National Oceanic and Atmospheric Administration's Coastal Change Analysis Program has developed aerial photography specifications for mapping submerged aquatic beds in coastal regions (Dobson et al. 1995). June is the recommended flying time for submersed rooted vascular plants in the Northeast.

The original intention of this project was to survey the eelgrass beds in June 2005, but weather conditions during the best tides for eelgrass detection were unfavorable and given such a small window of data acquisition (tide- and time-limited), it was not possible to collect suitable photography, so the project was delayed. In 2006, the Service was able to acquire 1:20,000 true color aerial photography captured during low tide on June 16, 2006. This is four years later than the photographs of the original survey that was captured on June 18, 2002. Figure 2 shows an example of a portion of one aerial photo used in this study.

Figure 2. Portion of 2006 true color aerial photo showing eelgrass beds (dark-colored areas) in Niantic Bay (enlarged; original scale 1:20,000).

Eelgrass Database Construction

Aerial photographs were scanned to create digital images for interpretation. Digital imagery was interpreted on-screen by an experienced photointerpreter who delineated eelgrass beds and created a digital database of these beds. Three categories of aquatic beds were initially identified: 1) eelgrass beds, 2) areas where eelgrass beds were suspected to exist, and 3) areas that had aquatic vegetation but not eelgrass. This aquatic bed database was forwarded to field personnel for preparation of maps to review in the field. Based on review comments, aerial photos were re-examined, needed revisions made, and the eelgrass database was finalized. In some cases, very small beds that were identified during the field survey were mapped as points and buffered to yield a polygon of 0.08-acre in size.

Field Work

Using geographic information system (GIS) technology, the field crew imported the draft digital eelgrass layer and superimposed bed locations on digital NOAA navigation charts. The combined data were used to produce charts for locating specific beds in the field (Figure 3).

Field personnel attempted to visit as many of the delineated areas as possible given time, budget, and weather constraints. Some field sites were far removed from shorelines or other visual reference points, making them difficult to locate. On-board global positioning system (GPS) navigation units were used in combination with the maps to find these beds. The entire breadth of individual eelgrass beds was not assessed; several points were evaluated within the mapped beds. Emphasis was placed on locating the limits of the beds that appeared to have changed since the 2002 survey and on looking in neighboring deep water for extensions of the beds beyond that which could be photointerpreted. While conducting field reviews, some eelgrass beds that had not been interpreted were found including a few robust eelgrass beds in deep water on the south side of Fishers Island.

Biologists estimated the density of eelgrass in the beds by eye from the boat (Figure 4) or by area observation using an underwater camera (Figure 5). An underwater video camera mounted on an aluminum pole was used to examine potential eelgrass beds where beds or bottoms were not visible from the boat. The underwater camera was used the majority of time. Exceptions to this were clear shallow waters where the bottom could be easily seen from the boat, very shallow waters where an inflatable dingy was required for access, and other locations where investigators could easily walk in shallow water at low tide and observe the substrate. Where necessary, a view tube (plastic tube about 4 inches in diameter and 3 feet long with clear lens on one end) was used to view the bottom and the presence or absence of eelgrass.

Figure 3. Example of eelgrass survey chart used to locate beds that were photointerpretation by NWI staff. The areas outlined in pink on the map shows beds in Niantic Bay that are also shown on the aerial photograph in Figure 2.

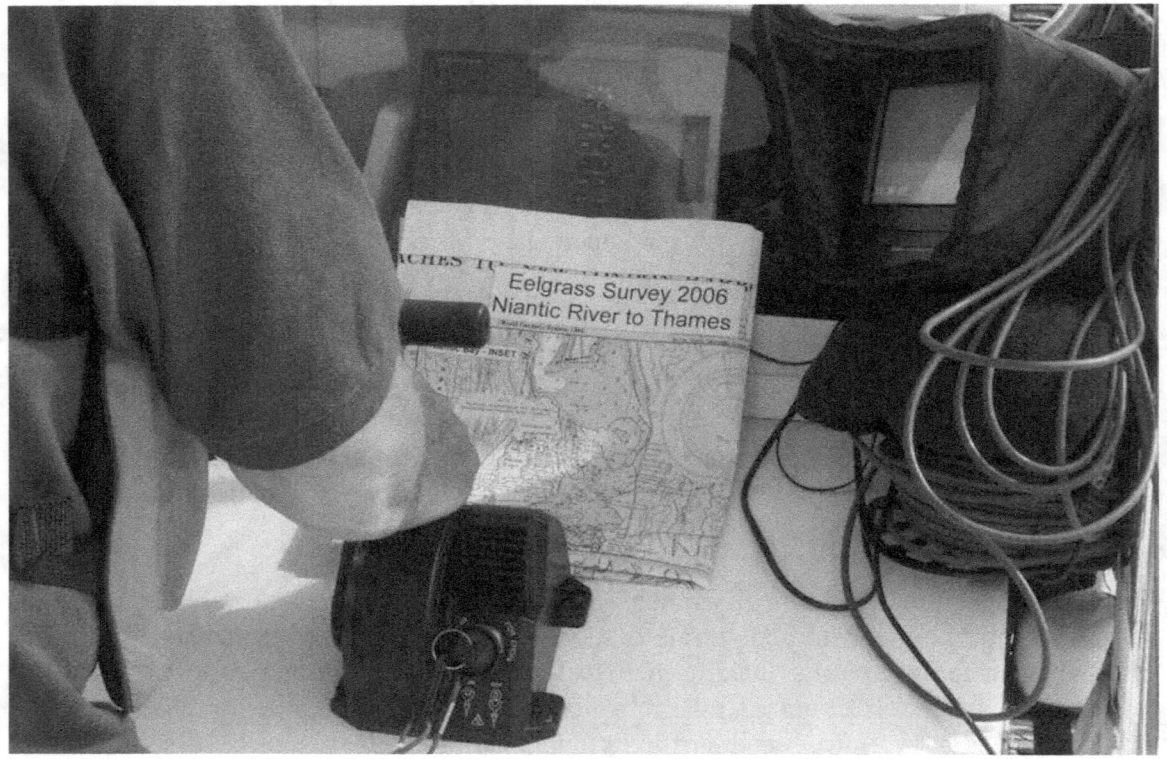

Figure 4. View of eelgrass bed from boat.

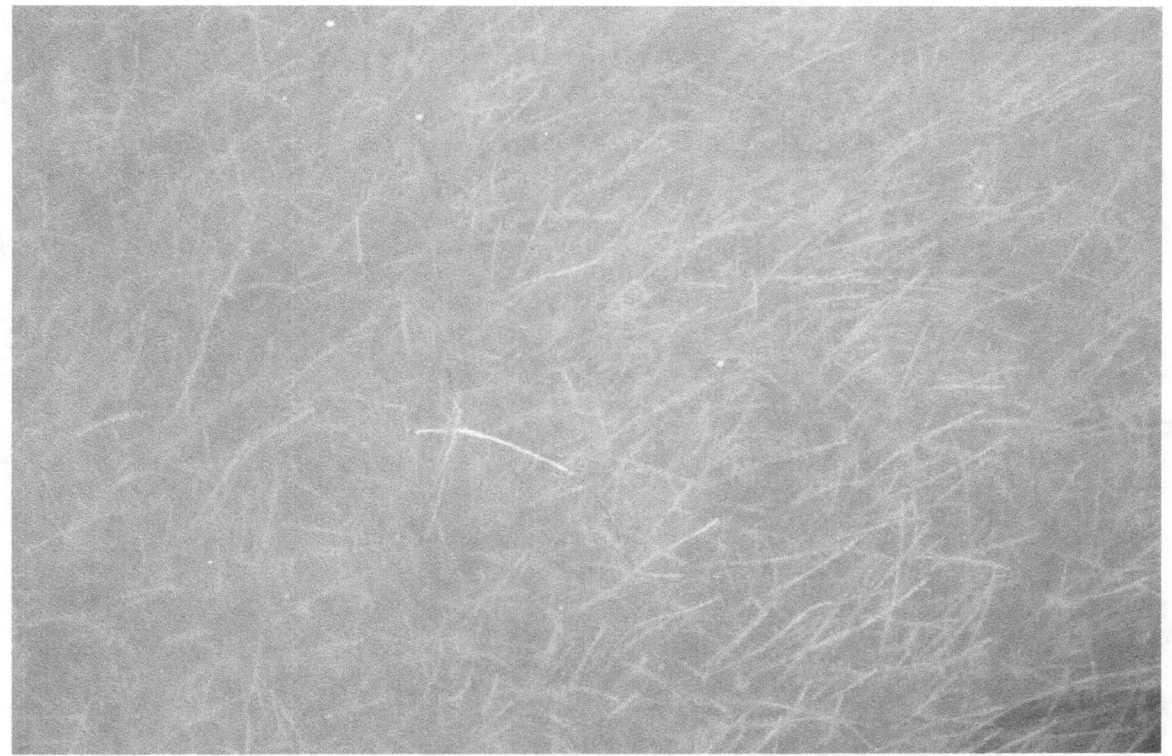

Figure 5. Underwater view of eelgrass bed.

No quantitative analysis of stem density was performed. Eelgrass beds were placed in three general cover categories based on relative density of eelgrass leaves derived by visual inspection: high, medium, and low. A sample of the field form is presented as Figure 6.

Field work was performed by Service personnel from the Southern New England Coastal Program Office (SNEP). Twelve days were spent in the field verifying locations of potential eelgrass beds during the late summer and fall of 2006 (Table 1). A total of 290 points were inspected: 183 were identified as eelgrass beds on the imagery, while 29 sites were others not initially mapped. Specific coordinates (latitude/longitude) were recorded using GPS technology. These data were added to the digital database. No field work was conducted west of the Connecticut River with one exception, Duck Island and the associated breakwater. Also some areas on the south side of Fishers Island were not inspected due to heavy wave action and swell. Researchers from Cornell Cooperative Extension (Southold, New York) performed dives in waters along the entire south shore of Fishers Island and verified the accuracy of the interpretations (i.e., no significant beds were missed). Eelgrass beds on the south side of Fishers Island were impossible to delineate on the 2006 imagery, but since there appeared to be an increase in beds since 2002, point locations of verified beds from the 2002 survey were retained for this survey (Herb Bergquist, pers. comm.). Point locations of beds observed in 2006 were also recorded.

Table 1. Field trip dates and predicted local high tides.

Date	Time	Tide Height (feet)
September 21	9:20AM	3.0
September 22	9:57AM	3.0
September 26	11:56AM	3.2
September 27	1:08PM	3.0
September 28	1:52 PM	2.8
October 3	7:05AM	2.6
October 4	7:25AM	2.9
October 16	7:35AM	3.1
October 31	5:35AM	4.4
November 3	6:22AM	3.7
November 6	8:44AM	4.1
November 7	9:41AM	3.7

Map Production

Using GIS techniques, 2006 eelgrass bed delineations and field check sites were then superimposed on 2004 digital orthoimagery (for Connecticut obtained from: http://magic.lib.uconn.edu/index.html and for New York obtained from: http://www.nysgis.state.ny.us/gateway/mg/). These images served as the base maps for geospatial registration of beds (Appendix).

Figure 6. Blank field data form.

Submerged Aquatic Vegetation Field Data Sheet

Project: Eastern Long Island Sound

Investigators:_____

Date of Investigation: _____

Predicted Tidal Data: Time of High Tide _____ Height _____ feet

Field Site Data:

Site #:____ Location (lat/long):_____dd
  Map Name/State: _____ Estuary/Bay Name: _____
  Time: _____ Water Depth:____ ft Eelgrass Present? Y N Estimated Cover: H M L
  Other Species? Rockweed   Other Algae   Other
  Comments: _____
  _____

Site #:____ Location (lat/long):_____dd
  Map Name/State: _____ Estuary/Bay Name: _____
  Time: _____ Water Depth:____ ft Eelgrass Present? Y N Estimated Cover: H M L
  Other Species? Rockweed   Other Algae   Other
  Comments: _____
  _____

Site #:____ Location (lat/long):_____dd
  Map Name/State: _____ Estuary/Bay Name: _____
  Time: _____ Water Depth:____ ft Eelgrass Present? Y N Estimated Cover: H M L
  Other Species? Rockweed   Other Algae   Other
  Comments: _____
  _____

Site #:____ Location (lat/long):_____dd
  Map Name/State: _____ Estuary/Bay Name: _____
  Time: _____ Water Depth:____ ft Eelgrass Present? Y N Estimated Cover: H M L
  Other Species? Rockweed   Other Algae   Other
  Comments: _____
  _____

Results

Field Review

A total of 176 eelgrass beds were interpreted and 126 were verified in the field (Table 2). (Note: Time and budget did not allow for all beds to be examined; this was also beyond the project scope of work.)

Table 2. Number of eelgrass beds in each sub-basin and number verified; other beds were not field-checked.

Sub-basin Eelgrass	# Beds Mapped	#Beds Verified	Sub-basin	# Beds Mapped	# Beds Verified
Fishers Island (NY)	42	29	Goshen Cove	8	4
Mystic Harbor	12	7	Palmer-West Cove	4	2
Quiambog Cove	16	10	Stonington Harbor	12	8
Jordan Cove	3	2	New London Harbor	8	8
Niantic Bay	13	12	Duck Island Roads	2	2
Little Narragansett Bay	11	10	Mumford Cove	8	7
Paquonock River	5	5	North Shore (NY)	3	3
Plum Island (NY)	1	1	Rocky Neck State.Park	28	16

Field observations about water depth at which eelgrass was observed relative to predicted high tide are summarized for selected areas in Table 3. Eelgrass beds were found at water depths ranging from 0.0 feet (exposed at extreme low spring tide) to 18.0 feet (Site 219). The deepest reading came within 4 hours of predicted high tide and the predicted tide for the day of inspection was 3.2 feet for that area.

Table 3. Examples of observed water depth for eelgrass beds in eastern Long Island Sound. Note: Tide predictions are based on expected tide reported for location closest to sampled eelgrass site. Predicted values for sites are mostly within 1.0 foot and 1/2 hour of predicted values for New London. Of course, the actual time and height of tide on day of record varies due to weather conditions. (Source data for predicted tide: http://www.tidelinesonline.com)

Site #	Study Sub-basin	Depth of Eelgrass (feet)	Time Observed	Time of High Tide	Height of High Tide (feet)
118	Stonington Harbor	3.0	2:30PM	6:22AM	3.7
116	Mystic Harbor	6.0	2:28PM	5:58PM	4.2
186	Mystic Harbor	10.0	2:47PM	1:08PM	3.0
108	New London	8.0	1:48PM	1:30PM	2.6
219	Fishers Island	18.0	3:30PM	11:56AM	3.2
211	Fishers Island	6.0	11:36AM	11:56AM	3.2
1132	Fishers Island	11.0	11:42AM	9:57AM	3.0
137	Fishers Island	9.0	2:00PM	9:57AM	3.0
171	Niantic Bay	9.0	10:36AM	7:35AM	3.1
New	Duck Island Roads	5.0	10:52AM	5:35AM	4.4
72e	Jordan Cove	7.0	11:23AM	7:25AM	2.9

Extent of Eelgrass

A total of 176 eelgrass beds accounting for 1,905 acres were inventoried. A summary of their locations by sub-basin is given in Table 4. Figure 5 shows the location of eelgrass beds in the study area. More detailed maps showing the location, size, and shape of these beds in each sub-basin and location of field check sites are presented in the Appendix.

Most of the sites with eelgrass were estimated to have medium stem density (Table 4). Only 172.7 acres of high density beds were inventoried. Please note that the density estimates are subjective and not based on quantitative analysis of cover.

Seven sub-basins had over 100 acres of eelgrass beds. Quiambog Cove had the most acreage with 428 acres. Three other areas had over 200 acres of eelgrass: Little Narragansett Bay (283), Niantic Bay (269), and Fishers Island (201). The remaining sub-basins with more than 100 acres of beds were Goshen Cove (152), Mystic Harbor (141), and Rocky Neck State Park (111).

Table 4. Eelgrass beds in eastern Long Island Sound in 2006. Sites are in Connecticut, except where noted otherwise.

Sub-basin	Acres of High Density (number)	Acres of Medium Density (number)	Acres of Low Density (number)	Total Acres (number)
Little Narragansett Bay	0	283.0 (11)	0	283.0 (11)
Stonington Harbor	0	66.7 (11)	4.1 (1)	70.8 (12)
Quiambog Cove	65.5 (2)	343.7 (12)	18.7 (2)	427.9 (16)
Mystic Harbor	73.8 (4)	37.9 (4)	29.1 (4)	140.8 (12)
Palmer-West Cove	0	34.9 (4)	0	34.9 (4)
Mumford Cove	0	75.2 (8)	0	75.2 (8)
Paquonock River	20.9 (2)	4.4 (2)	1.9 (1)	27.2 (5)
New London Harbor	0.1 (1)	24.3 (5)	10.1 (2)	34.5 (8)
Goshen Cove	0.4 (1)	142.5 (6)	9.2 (1)	152.1 (8)
Jordan Cove	0	36.8 (3)	0	36.8 (3)
Niantic Bay	0	267.0 (12)	1.9 (1)	268.9 (13)
Rocky Neck State Park	7.9 (1)	86.1 (22)	16.5 (5)	110.5 (28)
Duck Island Roads	0	0	6.4 (2)	6.4 (2)
Fishers Island, NY	4.1 (12)	190.4 (25)	6.8 (5)	201.3 (42)
North Shore, NY	0	18.1 (2)	6.8 (1)	24.9 (3)
Plum Island, NY	0	9.5 (1)	0	9.5 (1)
Total	172.7 (23)	1,620.5 (128)	111.5 (25)	1,904.7 (176)

Figure 5. General distribution of eelgrass in eastern Long Island Sound based on a 2006 survey by the U.S. Fish and Wildlife Service.

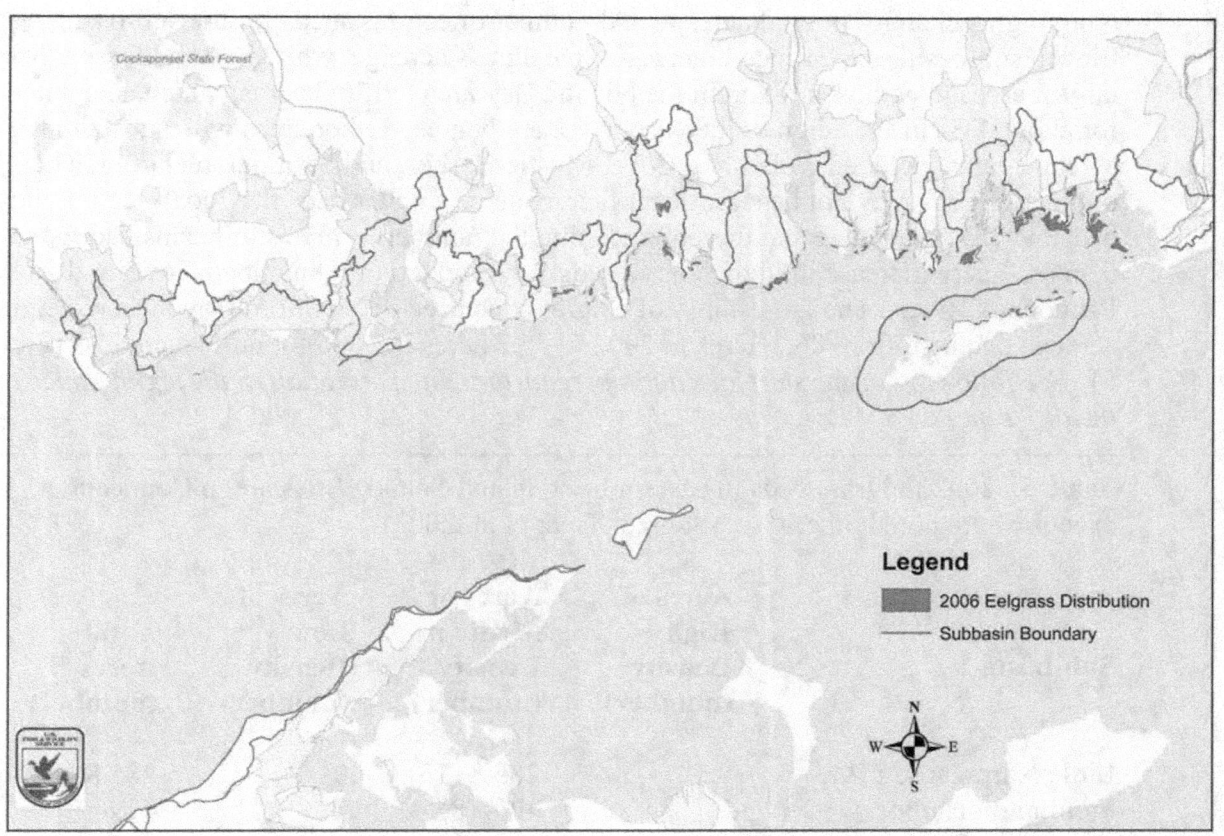

Comparison with 2002 Survey

When comparing 2006 findings (Table 3) with 2002 survey results (Table 5), we see that a total of 13 more beds and 306 more acres of eelgrass beds were detected in 2006. Table 6 highlights changes in total acreage and number of eelgrass beds for the sub-basins. Eleven sub-basins experienced increases in eelgrass acreage, while five had losses. The largest acreage gain was found in the Niantic Bay area (+130.2 acres) which accounted for about 43% of the eelgrass increase in the study area. Other areas with substantial acreage gains included Quiambog Cove, Mystic Harbor, and Stonington Harbor. The number of beds may not be significant feature since smaller beds may coalesce into larger beds increasing acreage and thereby reducing the number. Three sub-basins had more than a 20-acre increase in high density beds: Mystic Harbor, Quiambog Cove, and Paquonock River. The largest loss of eelgrass occurred in Mumford Cove where eelgrass acreage declined from 86.2 acres in 2002 to 75.2 acres in 2006 for an 11-acre loss (Figure 6). *See following discussion for cautions regarding interpretation of the significance of the differences.*

Table 5. 2002 Eelgrass beds in eastern Long Island Sound. Sites are in Connecticut, except where noted otherwise. (Source: Tiner et al. 2003)

Sub-basin	Acres of High Density (number)	Acres of Medium Density (number)	Acres of Low Density (number)	Total Acres (number)
Little Narragansett Bay	0	285.8 (13)	0	285.8 (13)
Stonington Harbor	0	42.8 (8)	0	42.8 (8)
Quiambog Cove	1.0 (1)	356.2 (9)	0	357.2 (10)
Mystic Harbor	0	78.9 (12)	0	78.9 (12)
Palmer-West Cove	0	34.8 (6)	0	34.8 (6)
Mumford Cove	0	86.2 (9)	0	86.2 (9)
Paquonock River	0	30.1 (6)	0	30.1 (6)
New London Harbor	0.2 (1)	23.3 (5)	7.1 (1)	30.6 (7)
Goshen Cove	1.7 (3)	73.3 (3)	82.0 (2)	157.0 (8)
Jordan Cove	0	19.2 (6)	24.1 (1)	43.3 (7)
Niantic Bay	9.2 (2)	129.5 (12)	0	138.7 (14)
Rocky Neck State Park	0	102.8 (28)	0	102.8 (28)
Duck Island Roads	0	1.1 (2)		1.1 (2)
Fishers Island, NY	5.5 (8)	184.8 (19)	3.2 (4)	193.5 (31)
North Shore, NY	0	15.7* (2)	0	15.7* (2)
Plum Island, NY	0	0	0	0
Total	17.6 (15)	1,464.5 (140)	116.4 (8)	1,598.5 (163)

*Beds listed as medium although no record of density was reported by field inspector.

Table 6. Differences in eelgrass survey results 2002-2006. + indicate gains and – losses.

Sub-basin	Acreage Change	Change in # of Beds
Little Narragansett Bay	-2.8	-2
Stonington Harbor	+28.0	+4
Quiambog Cove	+70.7	+6
Mystic Harbor	+61.9	--
Palmer-West Cove	+0.1	-2
Mumford Cove	-11.0	-1
Paquonock River	-2.9	-1
New London Harbor	+3.9	+1
Goshen Cove	-4.9	--
Jordan Cove	-6.5	-4
Niantic Bay	+130.2	-1
Rocky Neck State Park	+7.7	--
Duck Island Roads	+5.3	--
Fishers Island, NY	+7.8	+11
North Shore, NY	+9.2	+1
Plum Island, NY	+9.5	+1
Total	+306.2	+12

Figure 6. Aerial photos (2002 on top, 2006 on bottom) showing loss of eelgrass in lower portion of Mumford Cove. Dark colored areas represent eelgrass. By the shift in the small spit in the cove (near center of photo), it is likely that the change in eelgrass resulted from sediment deposition.

Interpretation of Findings

Although the results of this survey indicate an increase in eelgrass acreage, certain cautions should be made about interpreting these findings. In preparing this report, the senior author examined areas where the 2006 survey indicated huge gains and the one area of great loss (Mumford Cove). Aerial photos from 2002 were reviewed and the quality of the 2006 images is superior to that of the 2002 images at least in a number of cases. The decline in eelgrass acreage in Mumford Cove is clearly reflected in the aerial photos (Figure 6), while increased acreages may be real or an artifact of the method. It is highly likely that at least some of the "gains" in eelgrass acreage are actually the result of higher quality imagery or capture of the imagery at times of improved water clarity which allowed for more eelgrass to be detected. For example, a large bed of eelgrass in the middle of Niantic Bay is obvious on the 2006 photo, whereas no such bed can be seen on the 2002 image (Figure 7). There are very faint photosignatures in small portions of the bay where eelgrass was detected in 2006, so it is possible that the bed or some portion of it was present in 2002 (if these signatures reflect eelgrass vegetation). If this is true, then the bed escaped detection due to water clarity and/or photo quality issues.

Figure 7. Comparison of aerial photos for Niantic Bay (2002 on top and 2006 on bottom). Eelgrass beds are evident on the 2006 image and virtually absent on the 2002 photo.

Recommendations for Future Surveys

While the current procedures have offered a consistent, repeatable means of monitoring eelgrass, there may be ways to improve the survey. After mapping eelgrass in Peconic Bay and eastern Long Island Sound and doing a followup survey for the latter area, some questions remain. We were troubled by the difficulty encountered in trying to capture June photographs and wonder if we should expand the window for acceptable imagery to include late summer and early fall and how that would affect results. While June was the recommended time for eelgrass mapping in the Northeast (Dobson et al. 1995), the State of New Hampshire acquired aerial photos in late August for its eelgrass survey (Short and Trowbridge 2003). Also in mapping submerged aquatic vegetation in Peconic Bay, we used available October imagery and that imagery was exceptional due to excellent water clarity and high air quality (e.g., lack of haze). There are a few limitations of using October imagery: 1) macroalgae are often abundant at this time and may hinder interpretation of eelgrass beds requiring more field verification, 2) eelgrass density may not be as heavy as it is earlier in the growing season, and 3) by the time photography is acquired, weather conditions may hamper field surveys by boats. The use of late August or September photography would allow sufficient time for field work, but issues regarding macroalgae presence would remain and a question as to whether some eelgrass beds detectable earlier in the growing season would have the same density and shape. Yet, even with the June photography, we encountered some problems with macroalgae (especially on the south side of Fishers Island), so late August or September photos may be worth consideration. It would be interesting to capture aerial photography in both June and September of the same year to evaluate any differences in beds and photointerpretability.

The use of helicopter surveys to collect low-cost imagery and verify beds may be worth investigating as a pilot study. Helicopters can cover much ground in a short period and timing could be tailored to the best conditions for eelgrass bed observation (low tide). Also if successful and cost effective, it would make it possible to monitoring of eelgrass status on an annual basis. This should work well, especially since we've already constructed a geospatial eelgrass database for eastern Long Island Sound and a laptop with the existing data and imagery can be taken on the trip and used for reference and analysis. Capturing video images via conventional aircraft is another possibly low-cost option for acquiring basic data.

A final option to improve the results is to conduct a pilot study to evaluate the advantages that larger scale imagery would offer in terms of bed detection and estimating bed density. Acquisition of larger scale photos (1:12,000) or high-resolution digital imagery would make for interesting comparison with current techniques.

Summary

The 2006 survey located and mapped 1,905 acres of eelgrass beds in eastern Long Island Sound. Seven sub-basins had over 100 acres of eelgrass beds: Quiambog Cove (428), Little Narragansett Bay (283), Niantic Bay (269), Fishers Island (201), Goshen Cove (152), Mystic Harbor (141), and Rocky Neck State Park (111). Eelgrass beds were mostly present from Rocky Neck State Park east to the Rhode Island border. Four beds were found on the North Shore of Long Island, New York, with three in the Mulford Point area. No eelgrass was found from the Old Lyme Shores sub-basin to Clinton Harbor, except for two small beds (totaling 6.4 acres) associated with the Duck Island breakwater in the Duck Island Roads sub-basin. Most areas experienced gains in eelgrass acreage. The largest potential acreage gain (130 acres) was found in the Niantic Bay which alone accounted for about 43% of the eelgrass increase in the study area. This bed may, however, gone undetected in 2002 due to water clarity and photo quality issues. Other areas with potential gains of more than 25 acres of eelgrass included Quiambog Cove, Mystic Harbor, and Stonington Harbor. The largest loss of eelgrass was observed in Mumford Cove where 11 acres disappeared (probably due to increased sedimentation).

Acknowledgments

Funding for this project was provided by the U.S. Environmental Protection Agency, Office of Ecosystem Protection, Region I. Mark Tedesco was project officer for EPA, while Mary Garren and Johanna Hunter handled administrative matters. Ralph Tiner was the principal investigator for U.S. Fish and Wildlife Service (Service) and was responsible for study design, coordination, and report preparation. Herb Bergquist did the bulk of the mapping work: photointerpretation, digital database construction, and GIS processing and prepared maps and figures included in this report. The Southern New England Estuary Program (SNEP) was responsible for field review of potential eelgrass beds, with Andrew MacLachlan and Tom Halavik taking lead roles in this effort. Others assisting in the field included Herb Bergquist, Jaime McLaren, Don Henne, Greg Mannesto, Joe Dowhan, Elizabeth MacLachlan, and Barbara Halavik. Chris Pickerell, Stephen Schott, and Kimberly Petersen, Cornell Cooperative Extension (Marine Program), provided information on eelgrass bed location on the North Fork of Long Island and verified beds on the south shore of Fishers Island. Ron Rozsa, Connecticut Department of Environmental Protection, Office of Long Island Sound Programs, was instrumental in securing funding for this project. Aerial photography was acquired and converted to digital images by James W. Sewall Company, Old Town, Maine.

References

Dobson, J.E., E.A. Bright, R.L. Ferguson, D.W. Field, L.L. Wood, K.D. Haddad, H. Iredale III, J.R. Jensen, V.V. Klemas, R.J. Orth, and J. P. Thomas. 1995. NOAA Coastal Change Analysis Program (C-CAP): Guidance for Regional Implementation. U.S. Department of Commerce, National Oceanic and Atmospheric Administration, National Marine Fisheries Service, Washington, DC. NOAA Technical Report NMFS 123. (http://www.csc.noaa.gov/crs/lca/proto2.html#c4p1)

Short, F. and P. Trowbridge. 2003. UNH eelgrass (Zostera marina) monitoring program. Quality assurance project plan. Jackson Estuarine Laboratory, University of New Hampshire, Durham, NH and State of New Hampshire, Department of Environmental Services, Concord, NH.

Tiner, R., H. Bergquist, T. Halavik, and A. MacLachlan. 2003. Eelgrass Survey for Eastern Long Island Sound, Connecticut and New York. U.S. Fish and Wildlife Service, National Wetlands Inventory Program, Northeast Region, Hadley, MA. National Wetlands Inventory report. 14 pp. plus Appendices. (http://library.fws.gov/Wetlands/eelgrass_report_v2.pdf)

Appendix.

**Maps showing distribution of eelgrass beds
located during this inventory[1]**

Clinton Harbor/Westbrook Harbor/Duck Island Roads Sub-basins

Connecticut River/Old Lyme Shores/Rocky Neck State Park/Willard Bay
Sub-basins

Fishers Island

Goshen Cove/Jordan Cove/Niantic Bay Sub-basins

New London Harbor/Paquonock River/Mumford Cove Sub-basins

Palmer-West Cove/Mystic Harbor/Quiambog Cove Sub-basins

Stonington Harbor/Little Narragansett Bay Sub-basins

New York Long Island, Orient Point Area

---

[1] The quality of the base maps was not under our control; they do represent the most recent geospatial map product available for this area and were chosen for that reason.